Richmond upon Thames Libraries

Renew online at www.richmond.gov.uk/libraries

LONDON BOROUGH OF
RICHMOND UPON THAMES

TEETH IN THE BACK
OF MY NECK

TEETH IN THE BACK
OF MY NECK

Monika Radojevic

1 3 5 7 9 10 8 6 4 2

#Merky Books
20 Vauxhall Bridge Road
London SW1V 2SA

#Merky Books is part of the Penguin Random House group of companies
whose addresses can be found at global.penguinrandomhouse.com.

Penguin
Random House
UK

First published by #Merky Books in 2021

www.penguin.co.uk

A CIP catalogue record for this book is available from the British Library.

ISBN 9781529118636

Typeset in 11/13 pt Garamond by Jouve (UK), Milton Keynes
Printed and bound in Great Britain by TJ Books Ltd.

The authorised representative in the EEA is Penguin Random House Ireland,
Morrison Chambers, 32 Nassau Street, Dublin D02 YH68

Penguin Random House is committed to a sustainable future
for our business, our readers and our planet. This book is made
from Forest Stewardship Council® certified paper.

For Tata, Mamãe, Lara, Luka

Together you have given me everything

CONTENTS

THE TEETH

SONGS FOR NOBODY

I want
the clouds to crack open like an egg and
dump all their squealing water into our laps,
plaster our hair to our faces mid-argument
so all the fights that don't matter will be left with their mouths
    hanging open.

I want
the sky to do something drastic, even fatal,
like fling itself onto our shoulders so our heads snap up
long enough to recognise something is wrong,
and I want the bees and the locusts and the wasps to clump together
and fly erratically,
as if they were about to swoop down at us in an arrow of transparent wings,
making us feel so nakedly small and terrified,
that our feet refuse to work for us any longer
and they join the revolution, keeping us fixed and staring.
And I want this to happen now. Right now.
Some apoplectic wave must wash across the earth
and remove all the carnivorous mass of wrongness we have been
    gathering up
like valuables,
so that all the systems that actually twist and break the human soul
become so brittle,
we will only need to sit on them to crumble them once and for all.
I want
the ocean to invert itself and, like chewed-up wads of gum, spit out
all the plastic mistakes we buried inside it,
I want
the sea to vomit up the cancer and let it splatter like a blood clot onto a
    sand that will quickly
and quietly absorb it into yellowness and brownness so
new people with new eyes

will not see it or smell it or taste it,
when they come along.
I want
the whales to suck in bellyfuls of fetid air and sing their songs for nobody,
and I want the noise to be loud and unbearable,
trauma translated into a sound only the tiny bones in the human ear
    can pick up,
and let it become a forever-tune, like the sudden ringing in the ear.
I want us to flinch as we stand with no voice
and no feet to run
and our eyes betraying us
so they too do not shut, do not miss the moments when the birds make
no noise,
as they hover so close to the ground,
so close that they could pluck a single blade of grass with their beak,
if they choose.
And I want
one of them to *choose* to do it.
And I want that blade of grass to split the ground like an apple being
    snapped in two,
I want the dirt to carefully, lovingly, gently
return all the stolen labour, stolen bodies, stolen life
we have taken by
using entire races as fodder to build empires upon.
I want us to watch this happen and stretch forward
to meet the figures climbing out and shaking off the soil from their
    clothes,
and I want the trees to s l o w l y and carefully
pick up their roots, lift their long skirts –
and pluck up all the buried landmines with a
faux-genteel delicacy,
hold them between thumb and forefinger and
fling them up in the air to explode in heat and sudden stillness.
I want the shock of it, the audacity of it,
to burst open buried graves

at the same moment

lines of people (taken too soon)
gather to watch their own skeletons rise in silence.
I want all of us watching to feel our knees buckle,
like god herself was resting her elbows on our backs, watching the show.
I want her
to fling her arms up in the air, resolution lacing her brows so
the mountains give great shudders and sit up to stretch, to roll stiff necks,
to reveal themselves to be sleeping giants.
I want them to bend over and clamp blunt teeth into the backs of our
    necks,
the way a lioness picks up her lion cub with precise tenderness,
and I want our limbs to dangle for a moment
over the pit of our stink before we are deposited on the precipice of a
    volcano,
able only
to stare at each other.
I want us
to take deep breaths,
let that ash settle like fine dust in the rims of our eyes, darken our gums,
    embed into the
foetus curls of our ears,
and start coughing up our damage, coughing it up so aggressively
that we lose control of our own bodies and surrender,
as we pretend to sleep,
held hostage by a virus that chews up holes in our lungs.

These moments, they bite. They have legs. They live in our mattresses
and creep up to sit on our eyelashes at night.
I want the earth to watch us watching it, and to come to a sudden and
    jolted decision
to wrap this rot
in a thick bin liner,
and deposit it under each of our beds,

lest we try to forget
and edge towards the before times.
When the chaos, still, was written
but invisible to most.

CAKE

Cake is bitter when forced down your throat,
as you walk down the street – your street, your home turf – unguarded
and seconds later a comment makes the morning laughter choke off.
Now that road is forever a battle ground.
These thoughts are masked in a particular sugary smell that follows
     you up into the train station,
makes you feel like the ground is unbalanced under your feet only,
makes you question if what you heard was more innocent than
what the clench in your gut tells you,
(makes you wonder if anyone else can see insecurity clawing at your neck?)
You stand in between bodies and let the moment run through you:
     endless loops, uninvited playlist.

Cake is sickeningly sweet when smeared suggestively across your lips,
by a man you don't know,
who generously shared his thoughts about what your skin must look
     like under all
those clothes,
as your body becomes a foreign body, fruit ripe for picking,
the strangeness of your exotic smell,
now so heavy, so weighed down are you by flour and sugar and milk,
the batter groans and stirs and
words are so unfamiliar all of a sudden.
So you meet thick air with silence
and the moment goes unchallenged.

Cake is arid, dust hard to swallow
when you explain many, many times that you don't like icing, and
they tell you,
you look like a person who would like icing,
so better shove it down a grateful mouth and wash it down with water –
(I am so exhausted of seeing this because
we should be getting better

at knowing when to stop).
Cake is paste smeared across a hidden eggshell skull and
fragility is not your friend here, so you keep a composed face,
pretend it doesn't matter,
pretend there's nothing to get over
(pretend it will not be carried on the sharpness of your elbows for
    many years to come).
You must tread so lightly these days because complaining only makes
    the batter thicker –
cake stains your fabrics;
but
you get up, you move on, sometimes you forget.
And when least expected,
cake comes back up the throat,
maybe as you're sitting with people you always felt safe with
and a thoughtless comment is loosened from tight lips,
maybe even from your own.
Ignorance always demands pounds of flesh you aren't prepared to give
isn't that why the fatigue runs so deep?

And finally,
cake is hardest to endure
when you see it lining the oesophagus
of someone you love.
When you recognise this is not a battle you can fight,
but it is a battle you must watch them lose.
No one wins when gritty sugar comes out to churn the stomach
(but oh baby it hurts the most when you see it, when you feel it,
the churning stomach of someone you need to protect).
And you knew it then, you know it now,
cake is unconsenting and its sugar drills holes into bones,
it is the spiky taste of disgust, of shame, of hatred that runs on empty
    fumes,
a comment designed to shrink you by cutting you off at the knees.
Why is it cake,
cancer wrapped in sweetness, coated in innocence and

birthday-party joy,
served up smiling when you are relaxed and no longer sleep-walking
     through life,
why is it *this* that scratches up the surface of the soul?
A numbness most keenly felt
as you keep a blank face and say you're okay,
(you lie)
as they keep a blank face and they say they're okay
(they lie)
while the decay sinks into the ground
and follows you home.

MEN WHO HOWL AT THE MOON

They hold big teeth, the men who howl.
They hold sweaty weakness in the sweaty palms of their hands and
keep their fists clenched tight so that none of us can see it.
They make big decisions, the men who howl,
they make them with words with jagged edges, cut sharp by sharp thoughts,
so all of us must wrap ourselves in fluffy cotton wool to insure our
    bodies from damage.
Usually that doesn't work.
They are bolstered by the women that love them, the men who howl.
Adored by a mother or a wife or something sexual in between,
they are propped up by the playground of injustice,
a see-saw so corrupt its wood has splintered, ready to embed into the
    softness of skin.
Such a perfume, these women emit, to keep them sedated, more or less.
They hurt in ways that change one's smile, the men who howl.
They hurt in packs of jacked-up rage, they rip big holes into humans with
    their big teeth and
their big decisions and they zip up their transgressions and zip them into
    nothing.
So nothingness becomes a void in
which their thoughts must live, to do these nothing acts, to nothing
    people.
They allow no challenge to their authority, the men who howl.
They put a swift stop to this with their hardened bodies and their
    hardened brotherhood,
they do this with the hardened insecurity they try to bury in acts of
    alarming anger,
and they tell us it's our fault. Throw us around.
They are rigid in their thoughts, the men who howl.
They do not like the other men that confuse them, and so one must be
    put in one's place
before one turns into one hundred,
and their loud world loudly falls apart.

And so,
we die at the hands of the men who howl, we die because we fight
        back with crooked backs,
crooked from the holding of the scales heavy with the weight of
        their teeth,
or because
we are simply there when they decide to bite.
We reap what we sow,
howl the men who howl at the moon. They remind us,
we reap the misery that misery sows and eat it for breakfast, eat it until
        it has eaten us into
muted and drifting creatures,
nothing to lose means everything to gain and so,
they are afraid, the men who howl at the moon. They know.
Slowly slowly, we are the roots that grow the vines that trap their feet,
the men who howl at the moon.

TO BE A WOMAN

To be a woman is to be mute.
Make no fuss, shout no poison. This is what I've been told since the
 beginning:
that life is a race and to be a woman is to start tongue-tied.
No one asks me how I feel about that,
so I learn to carry this flint inside my heart:
we all already know,
to be a woman is to hide rage and all that makes us human.
Gift-wrap it, swaddle it in silk, and hang it up on the wall like art.

To be a woman is to always be demanding:
I don't need reminding that *some* things are getting a *little* better,
for a *handful* –
I cut my teeth on better,
and better isn't good enough.
Why do you knock pegs into progress, make us hang it on a washing line,
and pat yourselves on the back?
As with that same grin, you cut off our oxygen,
then gather amongst yourselves to discuss everything we steal from you.
Perhaps you fear the Medusa that sits within each of our faces,
and shrink back from the heat that snakes through our blood.

To be a woman
is to be the 'almost there' walking into every room,
and everyone loves to roll their eyes at her fighting for her cause,
invalidate her as too angry, too selfish or far too dangerous:
leave her burning at the stake.
When commodity is gendered,
every single one of us must pay our way with our bodies,
in some shape or form.
Doesn't matter where you go,
that shadow follows you everywhere
and the people who say they can't see it, well, they're lying.

To be a woman is to always be a shoulder
to any soul that needs one to cry on,
doesn't matter if you're busy.
You must have a skeleton made of wire,
to contort and bend your way around others.
Then you must raise a skeletal daughter
and attach those same strings to her.
It is so comforting and so sexy to believe the milestones of the past
are the signposts of the future,
and emancipation sits with the sunrise.
But we know enough to know
things aren't changing fast enough to save our daughters,
and every sunrise leads to a sunset.

To be a woman is to grow up quickly:
perfection is a concrete slab that encases our feet,
heavy enough to make us stand very still,
as double standards walk in and out the room.
And we are always so undeserving of our own ascension,
attributable only to the hungry quotas or the sellable body.
It is forever demeaning that in order to move through
space unhindered,
we must douse ourselves in eau de fragilité.
To be a woman is to be exhausted.
To be honest: I'm so tired of being tired
from proving my self-worth with my voice lowered and my head bowed.
Our rage must always be palatable, our demands
always wrapped in flowers.
Why can't you take me as I am?
I learnt it the hard way, but I learnt,
to be a woman is to be one's own woman.
And with all due respect,
we don't need your space: we carve our own.

WHEN

When
the first trains rubbed against each other on soon-to-rust tracks
made from sweat and browning, broken backs,
women held pins in their mouths
to ward off the lips of men in the dark and musty carriages.
It was thought to be sensible to bleed internally
in order to
keep your body clean.
When
Jack the Ripper stalked the streets for skin to tear apart and claim,
for women to own, possess and maim,
word got out that all he killed were a few worthless prostitutes –
nothing to despair about.
(That rumour was a lie by the way, but the history books will tell you
        otherwise),
better to be dead than sexual, some say.
When
the speculum was first invented,
by a doctor whose contributions are misrepresented,
the testing of that instrument
was first forced between a Black woman's legs.
Patient unconsenting
and doctor unrepenting,
because lives run cheap when they aren't white,
as the ocean floors may remind you.
When
women protested in Tahrir Square
with streams of colour to cover their hair,
they told a second story,
of how the tongue of violence comes to lap up the female body.
As pain nailed itself into the soles of their feet,
and clothes were stolen from their limbs;
still, they marched anyway.

When
Hollywood opened its silver doors
to push out sinful women they branded as whores,
we saw several little secrets stitched into elaborate dresses,
and Me Too became a call designed to snap at the heels of men,
a whitewashed moment,
a hashtag trend.
Be wary with this momentary justice,
as it turns out,
even women who can shout pretty loud
are still strangled
by men who claim to love them too much.
When
it's dark and you are smiling at your friend,
and it's too late to change how this night must end –
no second pair of eyes to guard behind you
(black dress, short dress, no tights underneath)
and a hand slips up and under as if to electrocute you.
When
you go still, meet your friend's eyes whilst she talks and doesn't realise
this invasion you didn't prepare for, can't prepare for,
and now time comes to decide
which bridge you must force yourself across –
confrontation or
self-preservation?
Too late now anyway.
Because he's gone and most of all,
you hate the way he caressed you so gently,
as if he were doing you a favour.

When
we can walk home without keys clenched between fists,
and it no longer feels so heavy to exist,
when little girls are not forced to grow up too fast
and the weeds men leave are uprooted at last,
when I can walk into a crowded hall

and not have to stand with my back against a wall,
only then can I stop taking stock
of all these crimes this world has collectively forgot.

Our era is turbulence, and the scales may never tip again.
I ask you, if it's not now, then it's never,
and what then?

THE RIGHT KIND OF BLOOD

The right kind of blood
is odourless and never repugnant:
it is the brave blood
of the wounded soldier,
or the guilty blood
of the beheaded aristocrat,
or the dutiful blood
that coats a newborn.
It carries pain and glory
but never shame,
these rivers that run
underneath our skin,
written into histories
created by men, curated for men,
where women are so invisible
it is as if they never existed.
You see, the right kind of blood
is the good blood, the noble blood,
immortalised by countless wars,
woven into threads of the dead from the
Somme
or Rwanda,
or Native America,
or anywhere really.
Soaked into desert sand,
or inky earth or salted water,
or siphoned in tubes
to save a life,
to diagnose,
to medicate.
The right kind of blood
is *not*
the silky trails
that curl down the shower drain,
as you dispassionately
nudge the clumps with a pointed toe.
It is *not*
the rustic brown that dots the mattress
or the richness
of the fresh red on your underwear
that stares
when you sit unaware
on the toilet seat.
It is *never*
the glistening blood
that lazily smears
the inner thigh
after two bodies have entangled,
or
the sudden, angry burst,
a sneeze,
that makes you
jolt
up from your seat in panic.
No, the right kind of blood
is any kind of blood

17

that comes
except the one
Even Gods forbid it
lest the shame
to crawl along
sacrosanct walls,
lingers
No, the right kind of blood
(virginal, for example)
never the soaked rag
or the tampon string
Any blood
as long as it doesn't carry
of being from
That kind of blood
the most dangerous,
Bombs can fall
but still,
dries dark
These poisons
that caresses
to choke her
she can draw oxygen
and to
before
Allow me
The right kind of blood,
blood
as we walk around
It is the accidental smear

from any kind of orifice –
between a woman's legs.
on their sacred grounds,
snake down our calves
and up
and the penny smell
in the purified air.
can be female
but never menstrual,
buried in secret dust
soaking through toilet paper.
is the right kind of blood,
the outrage
the lining of a woman.
is the dirtiest,
the one with the most teeth.
and bullets can puncture
this kind of blood
in scarlet controversy.
form the invisible noose
a girl's neck,
before
for fire,
wither her thoughts
they take root.
to fix this.
is the
we shed,
muted in our discomfort.
on the chair

and the taboo
the secret shoving
the simultaneous relief
That kick to the back
a grin
Some of you
that this kind of blood
something in you curdle.
might recoil
draws nausea
of the throat.
I kind of like
your
dominates you.
a frailty
to the monthly swing
And that's how we know
is vaginal:
blood

of the workplace,
up the sleeve,
and profound irritation.
as we nail
to our faces.
might feel
makes
Some of you
at the way it
from the back
I have to admit,
how intensely
heaving disgust
Creates within you
unique
of menses.
that the right kind of blood
the most powerful
of all.

CHRONIC

Outside this body is perfectly formed, flesh smooth, cheeks plump,
    hair glossy.
Outside it is easy and makes sense,
only minor irritations bloom beneath the skin sometimes.
But.
Inside, you get up, you paint the same door in the same brown paint,
    over and over again.
You shove fistfuls of the same music into your ears; over and over again.
You smash your face into a pillow and hope the pressure permanently
    numbs you: over and
over again.

Everything changes when your body is a broken city,
whose lights go on and off intermittently;
and you must assign the damage a numerical value –
rate your pain from zero to ten,
the doctor says, contracted in to fix these rusting pipes and sagging walls.
How can you weigh the way
pain generates a low buzz in your ears
when someone important speaks to you?
And you nod vacantly to appear normal but inside you are twisting and
    turning,
trying to feed this monster that hangs around your neck.
What number do you assign to that? You suggest five and the
    contractors suggest,
yoga.

When your body is an abandoned fortress,
when outside it looks so fresh, so ready for a fight,
with creepers pushing through the inlaid brick
but the wood of the stairs is quickly rotting,
and you have neatly folded up inside yourself,
now that the pain makes you quiet, makes you speak in half-words,

makes you a bizarre and hunched-up thing, squirming whilst your
     limbs stay still,
and the world walks by you and waits for you to package up your
     discomfort in a small and
digestible thumbs up.
What number is that? You suggest seven and the contractors suggest
stress reduction.

When your body is a badly planned suburb
whose roads run into each other and every left turn is a dead end,
when you wake up at 4am with sweat cradling you, mockingly, and
     sourness rising in your throat,
when you lie awake breathing pockets of stale air,
unwilling to wake your clueless partner.
You lie there, you lie there, hearing the pain flow through your body
     and wondering what will
break you this time,
will it be the moment halfway down the rotting stairs?
Where you suddenly fall apart and
clutch the banister
to save yourself from falling, no words left to explain.
Will it be the moment you sway after no one offers you a seat on the train?
And the words come out suspiciously smashed together.
Will it be the way you zip up the jacket of a slow burning ache?
Slap on a smile and tell your worried lover you're fine.
Will it be the crack of your face as you hit the hospital floor and they
     rush at you with needles
as your dad yells your name?
What kind of rank can you bestow upon that?
You suggest that it is a ten. A ten,
the contractors say,
a little irritated,
at a ten, you would be writhing on the ground and screaming.
But you *are* writhing, and you *are* screaming.
It's just that the pain has learnt to speak
with an inside voice

21

after too many years of dialling down and scaling back.
But,
they insist, and you believe them,
that you wouldn't be able to bear it.
You bear it. Reduce it to a nine.
The contractors suggest,
paracetamol.

LOCKDOWN RHYTHM

Give me something better
so that I can walk a little lighter.
Give me a world that places kindness on a pedestal, where exhaustion
	is not the
perpetual state of being.
Give me something fresh; not the same old tired canvas where the
	daily grind is both a
status and a currency.
Why must I walk down a path that likes to extract and extract and
	extract from me
until I emerge with my blood running dry, to collapse on the sofa at
	the end of the day –
and cast aside all my aspirations
for the soft embrace of a few hours of rest before bedtime?
Give me something liberating,
so I can walk away from unhappy situations without fear
that nothing better will come my way.
I always said in another life I would be an artist,
see,
in my head, I'd already hammered in this idea
that artist doesn't make the rent
and a 9-5 is the only way you'll hold your head high,
better shelve that pipe dream before you dare to give it flavour –
don't bother with art, don't throw your life into a useless beat,
why is creativity only desirable when it can be mass-produced?
Well let me tell you something,
lockdown living has got me picking up my pipe dream, my retro-sweet,
and placing it on my tongue,
and now that fizzy electricity has settled itself in amongst my taste buds,
for glorious months,
and I've realised I can't let her dance out my melting door, not now,
	not again, not ever.
So give me something better,

pile more options onto my plate,
so that I might figure out what freedom really smells like:
I want a rhythm that is mine to change, I want a calling not a job, a
duet not a one-woman marching band
who can't even choose her own songs.
I want to wake up wearing purpose on my head like a crown,
not a luxury but a right –
see
at five years old, unclouded by what the money says, I already knew
my path,
I'm
going
to
make
things,
I said. I'm going to write and paint and throw my soul out into the
world where it
belongs, singing who cares who cares who cares?
Does this phoenix sit in the skull of just a few of us,
or must every human shed their skin of dreams to get a foot on the
ladder?

Give me something better,
so that I can shout a little louder.
A system that doesn't mould you into a body churning out labour like
a factory conveyor belt,
or turn you into a whore for money that isn't even yours,
but as long as the house and the car come through and you've got your
weekends in the south of France,
what does it matter that you've got maggots eating up your middle-
class insides
and a one-way social divide where the only direction is down?
No!
Give me something solid,
give me something that doesn't prop up happiness and joy on the
misery of others,

where the division exists only on the train tracks,
and everyone gets to taste the same dignity
with their morning-coffee calm.
Give me a cleaner world that doesn't force me to blacken my lungs
just to get to work,
and a pulse where worth is not determined by birth –
no longer measured at all.
Look,
I want to walk on my own moon! I want to orbit my own sun!
I want to get up in a world that isn't all about how much you can squeeze
      out of yourself like a fat, ripened lemon,
drink that bitter juice for bitter people.
I want to strut to my new lockdown rhythm, a beat that lets me be me.

Give me something better
so that I may breathe a little slower.
Let time sit like a fragrance on the inside of my wrists,
instead of a rhythm I am forced to chase, beats too quick for anything
      to make sense.
Why is frantic the undercurrent of the city pavements? Why must we
      constantly grapple
with time's unweariness, carving out pockets of respite,
when time is a product of our own invention
and we have always been its master?
Now lockdown living has slowed down our cadences and
unlocked some universal truths;
perhaps none of this is necessary
and all we need is a stripped-back living
where we are plugged back into the soil, rather than to each other's walls.
I know it's almost *too* seductive
to slip into the folds of what life was before. Our tracks have been iron
      cast for far too
long, even inlaid into our spinal cords,
and oftentimes we have no choice but to rush towards the money.
Just yesterday, I would have agreed
that this world is bound in marble too hard to carve –

but let me tell you,
lockdown rhythm has me reconfigured
and these eyes see idealistically once again.
So
give me something that enshrines me in love,
so that I can grow a little calmer:
don't tell me that what we've got is just how the world turns –
this system is a broken carousel,
time to grab it with both hands and spin it the other way:
revolution from the bottom upwards,
a way of living that doesn't force me to colour in between the lines
    during frantic lunch
breaks and claustrophobic weekends
that don't belong to us. Yes.
Give me something better,
for my new lockdown rhythm to rock me to sleep
at the end of a day worth living.

HELL WILL FALL APART FOR YOU

Even
hell will fall apart for you,
no longer is it a warning.
You have rammed kerosene-soaked rags down this throat,
and the air is burning from above.
What use is grade six piano when the fires
have warped the ivory keys?
Hair and teeth and eyes, they are ash now buried with
all the properties lining the earth where there used to be trees.
Plantations have made the coffee and the sugar bloody,
and now
this has soaked into the clay and the terracotta tiles,
metal and brick and foreign flavours,
what good will they do when the fires have shattered all the windows,
and the worms crawl in?
Everybody looks up and suggests something be done,
vote for vagueness and security to break tomorrow apart
like we are breaking bread,
and whilst you have been busy denying,
my waters have been swiftly bleeding, drying;
this body cannot keep filling up the carcinogenic holes
you all have made,
when you forced tar and soot into this belly.
Those photographs from Bali won't save you when the fires lick the
flesh off the bones of those too poor, too *small* to get away,
consume them like pale and shining powder
(the kind that makes the pupils dilate),
and their demise lies in your hands.
I warned you.
Even
hell will fall apart for you,
the little water that remains is anger filled with skeleton fish;
what did you think would happen

when unfamiliar substances are pumped into my bloodstreams?
You think you'll reverse your destructive pace,
panicked eyes will shred the tea leaves (unsafe to consume) and
    prescribe prayer,
but your voices will be lost in smoke.
And when the fires come to play
(and trust me they will),
they'll choke your money down the drain,
see, god does not hear the cries of those who destroy what is worth
    saving,
or maybe
god died
from all the pesticide.
See?
Even
hell will fall apart for you.
This body should laugh but my oxygen is fading.
I know you will destroy every inch of me,
and then,
as the last grounds of breathable air shrink to pockets smaller than
    a fist,
you will charge admission fees.

HOW TO WEAVE A CHAIR*

Hello and welcome folks,
I am *ever*
so
excited!
Today, we're going to *save the world!*
Today, we're going to weave a chair.

Step one is design.
You'll need to accept that chairs are Controversial,
capital C,
angry people will vomit all over you regardless of what you do,
so it's best to ignore any points of contention and think about design:
a chair must be both beautiful and beautifully unstable,
a sad chair, a heavy chair, this kind of chair does best.
Too many millions of hands will need to, absolutely need to,
plunge their fists into its cotton-candy fabric,
those poor chairless souls who must stand on swollen, septic feet.
So keep that cotton arid, keep that cotton dry,
and you – over there – scratch out those pretty words you appliquéd on
so carefully,
this is not a chair for children,
please don't play dumb.
This process requires numerical, financial restitution
(it's all about the numbers baby!)
Flimsy words won't cut this cloth, and it's not like we've got much time.

Step two is IMPLEMENTATION, are you listening?
Step two is step one on crack,
you'll need to come up with a plan –
what is the purpose of this chair that is so weighty and so steeped in
    misery?
Who are we trying to *seat*, I mean really *seat*,
I recommend consultation,

talk at those who need chairs the most;
the elderly make for nice glossy photographs, 'unnamed african
child' also
gets the pennies rolling in
(bonus points if it's a girl with a baby slung over her back, I like those)
but ignore the ones in wheelchairs; wheels make us look a
little bit unnecessary, don't you think?
Anyone who looks hungry, anyone with bulging eyes, make sure you
talk at them,
and carefully write down everything they say.
This is an important step called 'documentation', which comes later.

Step three is my favourite: construction.
Stuff the chairs with cladding that is both flammable and cheap,
we haven't got time for premium, for quality, we've got backsides
to aid!
At this rate, those rotting, chairless people might drop DEAD before
we're done – then could
you ever live with yourself?
So spin until you have woven something that is just about credible,
that will suffice.
Oh, it's bland you complain? Bland is good,
bland is both practical and purposeless, incoherently incompetent is
how I like it,
and I'm the suit that's paying for it,
so what I say, goes.
Now,
take your woven cloth and spread it nice and *tight*.
We need it professional, we need it staying in place. For that
I recommend a staple gun.
Usually we'd handstitch, I know you might be disappointed but honestly,
the kind of metal that is sharp and capable for blood-letting
works much better for this sort of thing.
(Filthy chairless people might take time to learn to sit, might ruin all
our precious work
before we get good photographs.)

So folks, you want something nice and sturdy,
something that takes the *heat.*

Step four is presentation.
Now, expect a deluge of tears, because
you've built something that is quite literally life-affirming, you're a hero!
There's not much to say about this part. There will be many who are
        jealous,
who will seek to tear your goodness apart.
These days everyone's a critic, so ignore the stories in all the papers,
unless their words are kind.
This is the part where you are changed forever, the moment when
dark women with blank faces and
dark children with wounds tracing their fingers,
will creep out cautiously from their caves
and . . . wait for it . . . *sit down* with exhaustion!
You've done all this work for them, these bodies with no mouths of
        their own.
You've built them a *chair*, pat yourself on the back,
you sweet, pure soul.

(Step five is documentation.
This is the part where you take the notes of what people wanted
when you decided to build them a chair.
You take those notes and you shove them in the back of your drawer.
Dust off your hands. Step five's a wrap.)

Good folks,
my time with you has regretfully come to an end.
Today you have donated your time and your money to weave chairs for
        orphanages,
moved by God or guilt or plain and simple humbleness,
you personally, yes you, have touched me, really touched me.
I will never forget your sacrifice here today –
thanks to you, people who've never experienced the basic human
        right of

sitting
will get to sink into the finest, average-quality chairs,
we all take for granted. Isn't that something!
Before I leave, I must remind you to pay the remainder of your fee at
the door, cash only,
and point out
how wonderful you all are here today.
Without good people like you, like me,
the world would be far worse-off. I am so very proud.
Good folks,
thank you for coming to my life-changing, profoundly meaningful
workshop.
Today you have done something monumental:
you have learnt
how to weave
a chair.

* Best performed loudly in a thick and generic American accent.

A FEW BROWN BODIES

What's a few brown bodies from a factory explosion?
But a tragic accident,
limbs taking up gutter-space,
and the camera lens zooming in on the old frail woman, watching her
    weep with TV-ready gusto,
leeching off her wrinkles and her brownness,
as she begs you to save her son –
perhaps a wild dog sniffs at rubbish in the street behind her,
What a view! What a best-seller!
and top-tier countries release a statement, apologies with a chaser of
    broken glass –
'Unforeseen circumstancesheartgoesouttovictimsandfamilywe'll
    beconductinganindependent review . . . no stone left unturned.'
All the while
from the ashes rises another dirty building built off dark skin, othered
    skin, whose
pain is easy to justify –
production is, after all, the phoenix of western progress;
this is how we wear our shiny clothes and claim we are so awake,
    so aware –
What's a few brown bodies drinking poisoned river water?
Opening pores for cancer to creep up and into the blood –
must have been there all along, officials say, nervously fingering
    builders' hats,
polyester suits sweating in midday heat –
but bodies stack up like packing crates and anger swells, threatening to
    burst its banks,
as top-tier companies pay out pennies in lawsuits with one hand and
    build more
factories with the other,
and the BBC panorama films solemnly, white reporter Taking This
    Very Seriously watching

young bodies splashing, oblivious to scrutiny, beside colourfully
        clothed women scrubbing fabric
in water that glitters just a little too bright –
is that the reflection of their jewellery or is it viscose and petroleum?
the reporter asks us ever so seriously
as the back of their doughy neck blooms unpleasant red.
What's a few anonymous brown bodies being trafficked here and there?
But an evil that we just can't get rid of,
regrettable but alas, inevitable,
a casual statistic a hundred charities can throw out when it's money-
        making time!
And those donations need to be pouring in heavy and thick like
        double cream,
to ease the purses open they'll use a brown image taken without
        consent –
'poor girl didn't even know what was going on, searching through the
        rubbish like that,
we gave her twenty dollars for her time – most amount of money
        she'd ever made . . .'
easy money lets the falsely concerned off the hook, helps them line
        their discomfort with plastic paper –
donate a fiver on your way to Primark
and congratulate yourself for Playing Your Part!
Then keep your head down because caring is not only a massive sacrifice
but it makes you a touch too unpopular at dinner parties
where some people slip Malthus down their throats after the port and
        suggest the
problem is *too many brown bodies* because that's *too many mouths to feed*,
just stop living your lives as you know them and putting children into
        the world for the *love of god* –
it's a willing blindfold,
believing colour is irrelevant to the way the bricks are stacked,
much neater to blame the bodies themselves
than swallow the mucus of complicity.
Meanwhile, others think
(very privately)

(very quietly)
that all that colour might be better off in the sex trade, at least then
        they'd have a meal or two
and some money trickling between their thighs,
I don't know . . . maybe they chose this to escape something worse?
After all, does a brown-bodied bird *really* yearn to fly free
when all it has ever known is a cage?

WHEN WE ARRIVE

I get up to wash my feet with water.
Feet that stain with weight and distance
each toe an imprint on the ground,
it's not my house but it's my house too –
I get up to wash my feet with water.
Whilst I can still remember the connection of the thigh to the hip, the
    knee to the thigh,
the ankle socket oiled smooth and painless.
Painless for now.

I get up to wash my hands with water.
Hands that drag and bump against my bones,
like they don't belong to me.
Today the water is gritty and smells strange –
I get up to wash my hands with water.
Whilst I understand the motion – the pressing of the soap dispenser,
    the curling of my fingers
around plastic, rubbing the water between my palms,
water that is clean,
clean for now.

I get up to wash my body with water.
The body that is all these shapes unrecognised,
is it mine or is it broken?
Today I hear the water is barely running –
I get up to wash my body with water.
Whilst I still have the urge to wash, an urge so precious I cry with relief,
this body is full of feelings,
feelings that don't yet unstitch the skin,
keeping me whole,
whole for now.

I get up to wash my face with water.
A face still swollen with the echoes of the evening
when darkness acts as not a blanket but a shroud.
A face that looks blank and feels blank for safety,
I see a camera and several uniforms today –
I start singing –
I get up to wash my face with water.
Whilst I still have a face with eyes and lips that open and shut,
and I still know how they work,
they're keeping me gazing and smiling
gazing and smiling for now.

I get up.
I get up to wash.
I get up to wash my soul with water.
My soul a wound that is pumping out nothing.
First it was blood and now it is nothing –
they say we're moving soon so I'm staying clean –
I get up to wash my soul with water.
Water, I am told, cleanses. It wipes away the sin and shame it wipes
        away the heart
I get up to wash my soul with water.
A soul that gets up every hour,
every hour for now.

They said
'she liked it that way'
and the courts agreed.
I too must concede, because I am dead.
He said I started it, this man with dirt under his fingernails,
he said it in the silence that stretched between us with my eyes glassy
and reflective, letting him see himself,
and spin it how he wanted.
He said it with purple violets blossoming on my neck,
with blood broken under the surface,
tapping impatiently against skin that still feels warm.
And the courts agreed.
And since the courts agreed, I agreed too I guess,
since I am dead and cannot tell them for myself.
Never mind that those who know me from the beginning explain,
quite desperately, that no matter what I agreed to,
I never agreed to die.
But a woman's word is worth pennies when she is alive
so why would it mean more in death?
They said

I degraded myself,
I strangled *myself*, that day I walked in with my eyes not darting to the exit.
Walking in means you don't intend to walk out,
they explained, guided by whispers from his hard mouth with red-
        rimmed, apologetic eyes.
Any woman who loves sex this much, this hard, this unapologetically,
what can you expect?
Haven't we known since the first wars
that desire and death are lovers intertwined,
and a woman's body is forever to be painted in her sins
until it is no longer able to breathe?
And the newspapers agreed,

they said: she liked it rough, that woman.
She was too happy with herself, too confident,
too comfortable in what she owned
and she liked to get it where she could.
Get what? the courts ask,
get what she deserved, they reply.
How do words of defence form when air no longer lives in lungs,
when hands no longer bleed for ink?
He said

I liked it, wanted it, provoked him for it,
and because I am dead,
it must be true now,
as if the luxury of fact is one luxury too far for the likes of me.
He told them I begged him for it.
We love to strip our women down this way, slip the agency onto their
      tongue
long after it has grown cold.
See – all he did was make a mistake.
It was just:
salacious sex gone wrong,
BDSM misadventure,
kink-tragedy,
delicious,
frothing,
pornographic,
death
with filthy hands around my throat – but remember, I was asking for it,
I am always asking for it they say,
and the papers turn to me for confirmation but I am dead
and my silence acts as affirmation.
He said,

'she liked it that way'
and the courts agreed.
So he gets to walk away with slapped wrists,

head bowed with the weight of all his own suffering,
his own sadness,
this poor, tortured man.
What a burden it must be to
hook the world's ear
and convince them I orchestrated my own destruction.
And the papers turn to me for confirmation,
but since I have joined the ranks of the others
whose words were plucked from windpipes
prematurely sealed,
my silence is his victory,
my muteness, my confession.
And as the world is so desensitized
to the women branded complicit in their own demise,
I am left to wonder,
when the sun rises,
which of you will remember my name over his?

JOGGING

Let's discuss
all the ways you diss-assemble
the gendered body.
And break her down into parts to be
served on a platter still cloudy with the heat of her skin,
for you to consume:
Eyes to tell you that she wants you,
Legs to give you something to blame,
Hair for you to pull too hard,
Lips to beg you for it.
You mentally undress her,
as she runs past you with earphones in,
pretending to be oblivious.

DIFFICULT

To little girls born with fire in their mouths:
beware –
they will paint you as difficult from almost the beginning,
as if 'difficult' were a disease afflicting the young
who do not breathe self-censorship.

Memorise the tactics they'll use to pull you off your pedestals
into those trenches
by turning you into hysteria-uncompromising
and rage-unquenching,
as they convince you of your own demise
and dial down your music.

Stay vigilant for the ones who are not your friends,
who like to slowly push you into dead-end corners
and strip you of the very heat that makes you such a threat.
They tend to do it with a smile and a hug
so you are momentarily tugged by your heartstrings to believe
and believe
and believe
they wish you well after all.

In the years before the world decides you are a woman,
keep eyes on the ones that pretend they already know what you are,
and shame you into thinking
'difficult' is a curse that isolates you into unlikeability.
This is a lie. 'Difficult' is your lifeline that will root you
against the ones that tear at each other almost as much
as they tear at you
and line up such a willing betrayal.

Those that swallowed the rules made by men, from the start,
will try to shape you into some Thing, nice and soft,

Someone who bows internally and often,
is considered such a delight in the world we live in. So
do not let 'difficult' become your enemy.
Every woman that draws salt from the sea has it branded on her skin
    somewhere,
that is how you know your triumph.

To little girls born holding power in their clenched baby fists:
remember –
not all those who hunt witches are men.

THE NECK

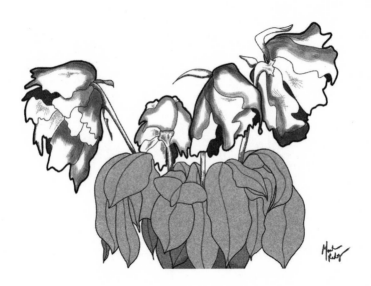

YOU ALWAYS SAW YOURSELF IN A CAPE

You have caught me; and now
I have to look you in the eye with the deepest of sighs
and tell you things are worse from that time –
that time you flew around the playground, bruised knees, clenched teeth,
pretending to be a superheroine, a Miss Incredible,
you who wanted to play Hermione in the Eden of the make-believe
but couldn't bear that she wasn't
the protagonist of the story (you always saw yourself in a cape).
So, you made Harry a girl and argued fiercely at the world,
the Lyra Belacqua of the migrant house,
constantly in trouble
for not doing what you were told.
You who organised classroom rebellions with hair still sprouting
proudly on your legs,
you who told strangers you'd rewrite the world
(back in the weightless time when
you *knew* you would).
You were the Violet Baudelaire of your own empire,
mischievous, agile, unapologetic
without having to be told.
(Why is it that most women want what most girls lose?)
I wish I still ran with the wind beneath my wings
the way you did that time.
(If only I could bottle your precocious self-adoration into a perfume
to dab behind my ears –)
I think maybe you'd be disappointed somewhat,
by my new Quiet and my new Conformity
(self-doubt is a language you didn't speak back then).
You'd tell me I am wrong to see the world the way the grown-ups do
(what do they know, after all).
You'd be so thrilled at the glow of me now,
this I know, because I know you well.
You'd look at me with an awe that I don't see,

and tell me to pick myself up off the floor.
I think overall
you'd be impatient
with my own humbleness and my own desire to be better look better
love better –
I don't think you'd recognise the sour aftertaste
of perceived inadequacy.

You always saw yourself in a cape.
And when you ruled this body,
you knew you were the best.

JANE

When you
let your mouth gape and fumble your way around my name,
and act as if it is the most alien thing
you have ever had to interact with,
or you
misspell it for the second time,
(third time)
(fourth)
in an email,
when I have already spelt it out for you,
I picture you looking me directly in the eye
as you take an eraser and slowly rub away each individual eyelash.
Then the brown mole that inhabited the corner of my mouth.
Finally, my lips.
So I must stay mute to my own erasure –
and then you wonder why I fold inwards
and hug myself away from you.

I realise that
this might be an overreaction
(I don't care).
My name walks into the room before I do,
it's my badge of (dis)honour,
my invisible birthmark,
my raised red flag,
that I might walk like you, talk like you, even smell like you,
but something about me is differently constructed
and you like to reshape people and their origins to what suits you
    best, don't you?

I know, I know, you like to let yourself pretend it sits easy on your
    shoulders.
We're good at keeping it mutual,

our pretending to be okay with things.
I see it in the way you ask me to accommodate
your inability to relax your 'j's, roll your 'r's, harden your 'c's,
as you bulldoze your way through a conversation,
and evidence your discomfort.
Seems surprising to you, right? That I might take something so momentary
and feel it like hot water.
What's a name, but a rubber stamp on the soul, after all?

It might seem small to you,
but when I was a child,
Dad used to laugh
at how I nestled 'Jane' into the middle of my name.
Tired of seeing me nowhere in the rows and rows of
glittered bookmarks and named bracelets,
I figured I would rebrand to fit a different mould,
a monosyllabic beauty at no one's inconvenience.
Maybe then my teacher of seven years
would spell my name correctly on my school reports.

I needed a hardened shell to place over the bruises
little punctures like that left on the skin –
and Jane was a heroine in her own right, wasn't she?
Swinging from Tarzan's arms to her own vines?
I guess I thought that I could imitate
that airy, freedom-feeling
those other girls seemed to pull directly from the air.
Funny how you feel it most keenly as a child,
that whispered hunger to be an English Rose
with lighter hair.

So, Jane was my casual camouflage,
picked to let everyone know I too had an unshakeable right to sit in my seat,
and I too could dress up like Disney

to smooth over my mispronunciations in the classroom.
You know,
the ones that made everyone's laughter take on sharp edges.
But Jane and I kept it nonchalant, wrote down all the wrong words
to memorise later, and proudly correct Mum
in front of others.
I hugged Jane close when I signed clumsy childhood documents,
pushing my real name to the edges for a while,
and pretended to be confused
at my parents' amusement.

23ANDME

Here's an idea:
a little bit of my spit will determine
which language I could be speaking,
what food I should be eating,
which box I will be ticking.
I have:
Borders pre-coded *into* my skin, I have
passports tattooed *into* the marrow of my bones,
I have ancestral whispers twisted *into* the drumbeat of my heart,
stories and smells and sounds
passed down through skin cells, from warriors
whose bodies are buried in jungles.

I can fill a test tube with chemical compounds,
and mould my flesh into castles without windows for you sir,
I can send the neurotic, joyful chaos that is ME
to a group of strangers. And pretend
I'm not afraid.
And they will map out the hieroglyphs of my history with pins and
threads made of wool,
stretching from ocean, to mountain, to river.
They will rewrite the stories I have
buried deep in the pit of my belly,
until I am gutted like a fish with bulging eyes,
and,
I have,
no windpipe,
left to explain to people,
all the percentages assigned to body parts – see –
my left leg is from *here* and my shoulder,
it's from over *there* –
as if on a butcher's table, I will prostrate myself and dissect
where I'm

free range and where I'm organic,
which parts are mass-produced and
what of me is inedible.

I will
regurgitate the deaths, the births, the weddings,
the celebrations I missed because
I've been trapped here, in the middle, on an island.
And they have moved on without us.
I will relearn the stories only half-told from my mother,
repaint my canvases until my colours
bleed together violently,
so no one will ever ask again:
what are you?
Because I shall have the answers!
Weaponised! Digitised!
and they will fix everything.
yes.
they will fix everything.

Just a little bit of spit, it seems,
will pull me apart at the seams.

So, I will swallow my own tongue,
and before anyone sees,
I will exit 23andMe,
and in six months,
return and repeat.

THE GREAT DIVIDE

We sit in the half-light, we sit adjacent
to the streams of hot gold, pouring through the windows.
Vovo cuts a pineapple – no – Baba slices a watermelon.
Flies patrol the skies like predators hunting prey.
Grandma, I say, grandma. I'm angry all the time.
Vovo regards me with her dark eyes, regards me like a soft, sage monkey,
fruit clutched between her paws.
Why my love, my darling, my soul of mine?
I tell her about
all the thoughts that sit heavily on my chest,
stone paperweights I fear will drown me.
And thus the great divide is born, invisible in the thick air.
Baba doesn't understand the roots of my rage.
You were born in *London*. You go to *good schools*
you have a *good father* she reminds me gently.
(you didn't grow up like me)
    brief pause while I ask my mother to translate a word or two.
    repeat to check pronunciation. Turn back to her.
I try to explain my fury when
men yell at me on streets they do not own, when hands I don't solicit
invade the skin and the warmth that hold me together,
when a stranger threatened me with that ugly, dirty act – yes, that one,
and I rooted myself to the ground knowing to
keep my mouth shut to
make it to tomorrow.
Well, Baba says, but sometimes it's nice to be complimented –
they usually don't mean any harm. I used to walk taller, my back
    straighter,
I used to tease them like you wouldn't *believe*, Vovo says
(you didn't grow up like me)
but grandma, I say, what about when their stares wire your jaw shut and
rip from your throat the words you have *always* used
as self-defence,

and twist them into origami silence?
Baba shrugs and reminds me that in life, men might be the head, but women are the neck,
we have to do the twisting softly softly so they don't feel it.
Tells me to pay attention,
to take another direction
home,
quietly.
(you didn't grow up like me)
Vovo tells me she was angry too, sometimes. But life does to women what distance does to lovers,
quenches that thirst, douses that fire.
She tells me our bodies must be our weapons sometimes,
we learnt to use them as *smokescreens*, grandma says,
scratching her chin with wiry, curled hairs.
      brief pause while I ask my mother to translate a word or two.
      repeat to check pronunciation. Turn back to her.
I say no. *no.*
I want my body to be
just my body,
not a weapon or a crime scene.
Baba swats a fly and hands me a dripping chunk of mango,
groans as she stretches out like a swollen knee
(you didn't grow up like me)
my love, my daughter's daughter, my joy, grandma had other things to worry about when I was your age,
I climbed mountains to feed your father,
I cleaned a thousand toilets to feed your mother,
I was taken from my family in the forest,
and the way back
rendered impossible.
I am not angry,
life is life is life is life, you know?
I won't know that, grandma, I *refuse* to know that.
Silence settles like the blankets grandma folds up every morning
on her sofa bed.

55

Vovo closes her eyes and lets the fan take over the chatter for a while,
and Baba's breath is slow, and even, and peaceful.
The flies sense their opportunity
and deploy the troops!
Attacking the sticky-sweet papaya husk,
the huge, swollen orange she had devoured in the morning.
(Vovo liked to cut off the tops of the oranges
and suck all the delicious, juicy pulp from its home.)
I watch her and count the lines on her face,
count the seconds between each slack-jawed inhale,
count the spaces in the great divide,
eagle-spread on the concrete underneath our feet,
and wish we could have spoken forever.

MY HOUSE DISMANTLES YOUR HOUSE

My house dismantles your house,
it's got three doors and all of my colours,
oh,
my house has markings on the wall,
my height, hers, his, recorded into post-blitz brick and wooden floors
Dad inlaid himself
one sweaty afternoon as the tar got under his fingernails,
so,
don't you even think about scratching it up.
My house dismantles your house,
it's an empire, a fortress.
When they signed for it
I couldn't even walk,
eyes untrained, so I missed
how the fear made their hands shake and their voices strain,
wallpapering calm over doubt and doubt and doubt and –
calling home to let anxious families know,
everything is fine. The kids are fine. The house is fine. The house is
OUR house and it's fine, all fine! We've made it!
Oh, that's the sweet relief, the smell of my house,
my house that dismantles your house.
Hung with pictures a wealthy man gave us,
my house is a palace, a paradise,
with my name written on the underside of the stairs,
unsteady pencil marks of a six-year-old, tongue-between-teeth
determined to stake her claim over this gold mine,
oh,
my house is the laugh of my mother,
the laugh she took from her mother,
the only thing she brought from home.
And my house dismantles your house,
it's a relic of perfection, a slice of something different,
where phone calls are loud, where Dad's volcanic vibrations punch

through the floorboards, peppered with beautiful errors,
in languages the neighbours don't understand.
Where every item is cherished as
solid proof
that coming here wasn't a mistake. A bank-approved confirmation
that the roots put down here were the right ones, the smart ones,
a price worth paying for their blood to have the right accent,
to carry power on their lips and opportunity in their mouths –
oh,
my house dismantles your house,
with its audacity and its pride.
It Fills the lungs and Swells the chest,
the lifetime achievement of the
phenomenally weary parents with their endless children,
immigration 'done right!' strangers said,
before they invalidated us with the ballot paper,
in sweaty 2016.
And now you question why Dad slams the shutters down in the face
of your discomfort,
but it barely matters to me.
See,
my house dismantled your house,
before your house
could dismantle mine.

TUESDAY MOURNING

This is how you tell us.
On an unassuming Tuesday mourning,
mid-hostile-commute,
with sleep still resting on my skin.
The earth might as well have been flat,
the way it dipped and tilted away from me
as my thumb scrolled through the 'Guardian', and I felt vicious all over
    again.
We were all unprepared

to read how under the new rules
parents and aunties and uncles and cousins
would have been sat across from an immigration officer
forcing them to count to seventy,
building fences between them, between them and me.
Well.
It's a special kind of haunting, a special loss of air.
Children like me

were raised on the bread of parental struggle,
where stories of graft and multiple jobs
are handed down like heirlooms
to sit against our necks: the immigrant's pearl choker.
I collect stories like drains collect rainwater, and heavy is the overflow
of collective disappointment
that comes from living undesired.
There's a price tag that comes with
leaving all their loves behind
and it imprints on the children they plant here as new greenery.
People like us

build a quiet kingdom
where we pick up the dignity

those who came before us
were forced to leave beyond the border.

And this is how you tell us. On a mundane Tuesday mourning.
Timed so that I must
slip into the office light
and pretend I wasn't crying.
Even though I'm safe from your headlights,
I'm a direct descendant of the villains of your making,
and pain is passed down in the blood:
daughters like me

were taught to be proud of our immigrant ancestry.
Nothing to hide in this palace of mine:
we learnt to drink your tea and eat your cake
and keep our music to ourselves.
Even though friendly wasn't the most familiar face,
as a child, I thought I was blind to it, mild to it.
But Tuesday mourning
brought back rushed memories I thought

belonged to someone else –
no warning for a brave face,
no time for an inhale to steady the sinking feeling of being so unwanted.
If your callousness were liquid,
we could fill our backyards with it.

PATRIOT

I heard it said
that patriot is a proud word to wear.
Claiming kinship keeps you rooted to the ground
when winds bigger than you come to claw at you
and lift off the roof tiles.
Bowing to the homeland keeps you whole, right?
It's held as a universal truth: you're honour-bound to love the country
    that raised you,
gave you a platform, and a stage,
and a passport to stamp out every occasion where you felt so deeply
    uncomfortable.
Even if that moment was the fleeting face
of the PM on TV.

I heard it said
a patriot feels safe in all their shoes,
comfortable that the fire in their home burns the brightest,
but,
is your home meant to fill you with shame?
Enshrine views that tell you to go back
go back
go *back*
from whence you came?
Or spit at the feet of your dad as you watch,
shaken to see the man you thought of as a pillar unscathed
be considered so offensive
merely for existing?

I heard it said a patriot drinks their country-love from the same glass
as their coherence,
so willing and so ready to close their eyes to people like me
who represent the crumbling of the old-blood order,
and feel this place sit uneasy on their chest.

You know,
not all of us can reconcile
this history that still spills onto the pavements,
pushed forward by veterans who only see backwards:
it's too much to demand respect
for a country that cannot resist
hollowing you out with how little it can bear to love you.

I heard it said
a patriot is an ode to that belonging feeling,
that beehive-buzz of cohesion.
But belonging holds a bitter aftertaste
when its entry criteria are so narrowed and re-twisted
by contaminated rhetoric.
2016 broke my heart in every kind of way,
but not much healing can come from the bigoted mouths of the
    leaders we elected,
who called for patriots to retake the control that they had never lost,
and pretended to be shocked
when the swell of hatred burst forth from the gutters.
You know, Boris,
the day after it happened,
my home was a ghost town filled with the gaping silence
needed to stomach this new loss.
We had to close the curtains to deflect the faces
of our neighbours, celebrating our grief.

And finally,
I heard it said,
a patriot sleeps deep in the folds of their delusion
that 'British' somehow means 'better'.
But nothing feels superior
about a people who felt utterly compelled
to make me an intruder
in the country of my own birth.

SLOW SLICING

So this is how
at eight years old
you mourn a loss that was never yours:
you tell no one. In your quiet corner, you pull out your grief and hurt like
the stuffing from a sofa everyone likes to sit on.
This pain is tiny but plentiful: the slow slicing into your skin
like a blunt hacksaw,
slowly. Slowly.
Death by a thousand cuts, inlaid with salty tears you struggled to claim
    as yours –
it's an ingenious way to live a half-life, carrying your loss like a
    phantom pain,
Slow slicing.
I've known it since the early years,
when I watched my loss turn every cry into an ocean, exhausted,
and we screamed until our throats were raw.
But it was always my fault, my fault,
grief is not a thing well understood,
especially not by grieving parents.
See,
they at least had each other to fall apart with,
I could see it in the way my mother cried and
the way my father had to shout to distract us from his broken heart.
I only had my anger to keep me up at night,
worried that if I went to sleep another loss might hit us again,
it certainly didn't knock politely the first time around.
So I kept long vigils over sleeping pain,
there's nothing like that kind of loneliness.
Slow slicing.

This is how, at twelve years old,
you mourn a loss that never happened:

you hit her. You throw your rage at her. You sink your teeth into
        her hand –
so gut-wrenchingly furious because you thought
she had sat up and swallowed the person you needed, you really needed,
one stupid afternoon, when the phone rang.
Slowly. Slowly.
And then things became
unfixable,
and no one thought to tell you until it was too late.
Grief is a many-coloured scarf that sits forever around
an uncomfortably warm neck,
which broke out in rash after rash
because you clawed at it when you were sad,
and you were sad an awful lot.
But a child's inner mourning is not a thing well understood,
especially not by parents whose mourning made them blind to tears
shed only when everyone else was sleeping.
Slow slicing.

This is how, at sixteen years old,
you swallow gunpowder to light the powder keg
of a loss that does not exist:
you argue that this burden was never yours to carry; you don't want it,
you denounce it.
Can no one understand –
you were supposed to be the younger one,
who watched the older one starry-eyed,
stole her clothes, listened to all her favourite music?
She was meant to lead you and you were meant to adore her –
do everything she did – because isn't that how sisters work?
I have no idea but I can imagine.
Slow slicing
until it hits the bone –
and then after that, what's next to go?
Slowly. Slowly.
You look back now and wonder how you picked up all your pieces.

At such a young age,
you carried immense guilt
because no one told you it was okay
to be unravelled,
by a strand of DNA.

CHRONICLES OF HER

To explain
what it means
to miss something you never had but always hoped for,
is like trying to understand the exact amount of quiet that happens
underneath the surface of an ocean wave.
An impenetrable, opaque window only I can see.
My sister is:
      my albatross
          my savagery
              my saving grace,
the spot between my head and my neck
where a single pinprick could kill me.
I love her,
but I want to reassemble her,
and for that I hate myself.
When I was young, and she was younger,
to try to build bridges over the chasms she created,
I weaved and stitched all her incapabilities
into a thick, oozing coat. And wore it like a mascot,
grandly announcing to everyone (and myself),
that as of today, I would take
responsibility for all the things
she Could Not Do.
I would be twice as brilliant,
twice as bright, twice as good at injecting happiness into my home.
I wore the coat until it exhausted me,
and resented her for it,
not seeing those threads were my problems dyed in her colours.
I decided she was doing it on purpose.
So I demanded a sister-like-all-the-others,
petitioned for hours of imaginary quests and,
powdery eyeshadow smeared across my cheeks,
I wanted video games and competitive stair-sliding,

lip-sync concerts and soap opera extravaganzas,
I needed footsteps to follow,
to learn how to love myself,
no one warned me that it was I who would be leading the way.
Greedily, I watched my friends lean their heads against older sisters
and fall asleep,
watched them navigate their space in quiet understanding
that *this* is what sisters do.
Mine gripped a pencil in her teeth so hard the wood screamed,
grabbed me by the shoulders and shook me until my head snapped
     back,
until I slapped her away.
She couldn't bear to be touched.
She used to hit me when I made her feel
inadequate.
I used to hit her to try and make her
adequate.
My sister is:
     my albatross
       my savagery
         my saving grace.
I protect her with my teeth, with my heart sitting exposed on my
     shoulder,
from everyone except myself,
she's the only one who makes me cry,
in a drowning kind of way.
Much like the way life turns down
the heat in our chests,
I grew older and calmer,
I grew more gentle.
She stayed the same, but I learnt to love her better.
A few years back, I swapped the coat for a lighter one.
Threads of acceptance. The colour orange.
We both like it now, it suits me better,
but the lining is still stitched with guilt.

CATERPILLAR

You should have seen her at her very worst,
an inbetweened thing,
caught inside feelings that lurched at her like a dark ocean swell
and thoughts that weren't so gentle either:
when the sun came to set and she looked at the face across from her at
      the dinner table
with food crusted on the corners of a strange mouth,
her words were sharp and hit hard.
To be honest, everything about her was steeped in a regular anger,
it might as well have been the dull ache that settles in the shoulders
after carrying something heavy.

This kind of pain sits unsettled on the barbed tongue,
both intentional and accidental.
Somewhat wild with a grief she knew she wasn't allowed to have.
You might have thought her nasty,
and to be honest, I would have agreed with you.
See, she always wanted a sister
but instead she had a caterpillar.
And this fuzziness, this smallness, this indescribability,
too many legs, too little space to run –
well they might as well have been the kindling buried in each corner of
      the house,
starting small fires everywhere.
It might be beyond the grasp
of all of you living on the other side of the murky waters,
where your siblings figured life out on their own, grew wings and used
      them to
float out the door into something new,
and you didn't need to cry on their behalf.
So if you can't possibly know what it means to love and loathe a
      caterpillar,
a half-formed subject of every single serious conversation,

everything circling back to her, to her, to her,
this girl understands your position of course
and doesn't ask for sympathy.

That's why I tell you, you should have seen her at her most ashamed,
growing up wishing for different, wishing for easy.
So that the younger sister wouldn't have to grow older than the oldest
   one,
and defend her from a world too hostile for everybody's liking.
I'm not certain that she had the words to express her extremely broken
   heart,
this girl whose footsteps pulled up the drudge and the sediment from
   all the water she waded in,
trying to figure out why her eyes were so sore from weeping and her
   hands so bruised from clenching.

See,
looking out for a creature so delicate, so prone to being crushed or
   pecked or carried away –
is not the kind of thing that lightens your steps.
It is a full-time job and I can't say this girl, doused in angry sadness,
enjoyed it very often.
You might have thought her spoilt,
and to be honest, I think I would agree with you.
It's a bizarre thing to wish so transparently for a sister,
and instead, to get a caterpillar.

AMBER

I wish I could enclose you in amber
to protect you from the spikes of the others.
Just like the time I was a playground warrior,
keeping you tranquil by shouting in all directions;
your first line of defence.
I wish I could redact the pages that sit in your thoughts, tightly bound
    within a fortress.
You grip so tightly to the words spat out by the people
who broke you so long ago.
It's like their ignorance impaled the inside of you to keep you ashamed
and untethered,
but their misery is all theirs, and we hoped you'd siphon it out of you.
Like so many things,
we were wrong about that.
If I could,
I would plug your ears with silk to let you close your eyes and dream.
So much of your time is spent in the place we cannot visit.
You float, alone, on your island
and we swim within our grieving.

I know this isn't really true,
but I tend to feel like your prison guard,
constantly hemming you in at the sides,
because you cry so much around me, and I cry when you aren't looking.
You see me now as you saw me then.
Stuck in the schoolyard,
untainted by the luck of the draw,
and maybe too greedy
with all the things that came to me, malleable, like water.
I know I am so often
the villain of your story.
I wish it didn't have to be that way,
but I will fight for you even as I fight to keep you encased in slow resin,

protected from the pollution
of this world that seeks to shrink you;
I'd rather it shrunk me instead.

VITRIOL

Part 1

Vitriol walks into my bar well disguised at first,
and so i don't spot his inky sludge that seeps from his footsteps to
stain the wood i will walk on, for years to come.
(it *hits* me later.)
He starts off slow, soft, laughing as i don't meet his eye, but like the
    tides that creep away from the terrified shore,
before the tsunami strikes,
he gets *loud* and *oblivious* to his damage.
and i am zipped up tight.

Vitriol is heavyset, and also a father;
he shows me his cracked children on a cracked screen as i cordially
    plug it in.
(i lend him my charger.)
Acid is corrosive to the skin and
i am scared his spit will touch my cheek –
Excuse me? She is outraged as she beckons me,
exCUSEme but he CAN'T stay here he's OBVIOUSLY drunk.
She cocks her head to the side and tells me i must make him leave and
    for a moment i hate her more than i hate him.
Aren't we supposed to have an unspoken understanding
that being silent is still the best way?
When one must drink sulfuric acid it is preferable
not to let oneself rebel.
Meekness is a weapon when Vitriol comes around and so here i am,
nodding and apologising.

Part 2

i square up to Vitriol. i am polite. i am quiet. i am firm.
i hand him his phone and suggest,

ever so tentatively,
that he return to his children – his children must be waiting –
and later i will bite my tongue and line my throat with bile for this sin,
i have placed a spotlight on myself,
as the audience look on, impatiently,
and i tell him *sir, I think you should go.*

Vitriol is not tall. He is pale and has big hands.
He sees me for the first time.
And i see waves i cannot outswim, because,
Vitriol has opened his mouth –
and if disdain had a smell, this beer-stained heat would be it,
i am smaller than i have ever been before,
but too late,
when you hold your hand out for a beating,
Vitriol will oblige, you stupid, uppity bitch.
Vitriol tells me he is going to rape me.
Clearly no one else has done it yet,
as i seem to think i'm so important –
i don't! i don't!
(my bar is brown, and made of wood. The surfaces
get sticky by the time my shift ends and i am responsible for
clearing up the mess, and i am usually excellent.
My bar has only one way to come in and out,
my bar is too high for me to leap over and scream and scream and
  scream)

Vitriol stands between me and the door.
His bulk fills up all the gaps,
so even i, as small as he has made me, cannot slip away.
i am on the phone to 999 but something show-stopping has happened:
my voice must have made it out before i did,
because i cannot speak and
neither can my lovely audience.
Glued pleasantly to their seats they watch Vitriol
describe the cobwebs that must live between my legs

(because no one wants to fuck me and clearly
that shows, but Vitriol will do it on everyone's behalf,
so this stupid whore will shut her mouth)
his logic is perhaps the scariest part, but
all i know is that
i do not know
how to see the world the way i did before.
Acid leaves a mark you see, and a mark you don't.

Part 3

When the police come,
Vitriol is wiped away. For now.
Acid always comes back up the oesophagus.
My female 'friend', Miss Previously Outraged, informs me,
They found a KNIFE in his BAG!
can you even IMAGINE!
and when wide eyes ask me if i am alright. i lie.
i go to the bathroom and allow myself two minutes. Two minutes is
	all Vitriol gets.
And then i swallow it down,
to revisit later, when it tastes like panic.
Turns out,
panic is acidic.

MIDRIFF

I would like to believe we are born guilt-free.
But it seems like shame grows in the marrow of women,
and like a fungus, feeds on the insecurities rotting on the surface of
    our flesh.
My shame sits on my midriff
(I'd like to show you but it is not flat you see)
and so, clothes are strategic,
hemlines have compliance quietly stitched into them,
confidence must never be loud, nor sexual,
on the underground.
I would love to emulate the harshness, the untouchability, of the
    women of magazine life but
my shame sits on my midriff and so tight clothes are ill-advised.
(I'd like to show you but a line of hair that is not soft nor light nor
    feathery spreads out like a
sunset on water, snaking down past my belly button.)
So instead I sit on the train with my legs determinedly open,
to perform my daily rebellion whilst men stare at the thing between
    my legs,
as if that is the thing I am supposed to be embarrassed about.
Let me tell you, I got over that a long time ago.
My shame sits on my midriff,
as long as it remains safely tucked out of sight,
I can meet your gaze.
(I'd like to show you but I might lose all control, grab a fistful of flesh
    and hate myself.)
Meanwhile mushrooms sprout at the base of my feet.
Honestly, I'd love to sneer at the obsessions we have built
to distract ourselves from rising tides,
pretend I, too, have avoided the trap of misplacing value in beauty.
But these teeth in the back of my neck, they hurt too much,
I live in the urge to pick up a razor every other day,

'The presence of hair is a powerful and political statement on every body
    except mine,'
I tell my lover to his immense confusion, watching my weight, no
    eating past 6pm,
because my shame sits on my midriff, me, the hypocrite,
Love yourself! I tell my friends, wafting away their insecurities,
like I alone can fix something too deep to reach –
Honestly, I'll trip over my words in my efforts to stop your self-criticism,
Pound your comments into the ground and twist them with my feet,
    the way I would a cigarette,
but god forbid anyone catch the softness of my belly,
I might just vomit from the shame that sits there.
(I'd like to show you but I really . . . just can't.)
I'd like to believe we are born guilt-free.
But this faux sisterhood I see on TV, so few of them who look like me,
become such helpful hands that mould shame into crowns, to be adored
    and adorned,
keep me sucking in, just a little, every photographic moment.
It is them I murder myself for, in the morning, in front of mirrors,
    with apologies for breakfast and regret for dinner.
It is the women who see the shame that sits on my midriff,
these women with teeth in the back of their necks.
I might just say fuck it and expose what I find so supremely unappealing,
to eyes that most likely do not care, it's just a body after all,
there are bigger problems and don't I know it.
I might. I might.
But shame is women's DNA to be pulled from their molars
and I am strong, but,
my strength is only relative to the weights that are silently birthed
    with us.
And meanwhile, mushrooms grow at the base of my feet.

IF I COULD

Our conversations are a game of chess,
and I have never known the rules.
Every single sentence
is a challenge, a barbarism designed
to slip under my skin and shimmy it off.
So my composure circles the drain and
you tell me you cannot speak to me
when I get 'like this'.
And if I could,
I would flatten and stretch myself to become your mirror –
but I am what you made me, my father's daughter, after all,
you raised me to be headstrong and
wear my beliefs like a crown.
You taught me to speak truth with my chest and
moulded me into something fierce,
praised me for my uncompromising steps through life,
until we discovered just how different I would become
from the kind of daughter you needed
to soak up the pain of your firstborn.
And if I could have done that for you,
trust me I would have, all those moments I saw you needed it.
If I knew a way to put out that fire I'd turn my
body into a reservoir,
and keep us in still waters.
I might have even tempered down
my thunderstorms to
be exactly who you wanted,
but you taught me to be unapologetic in your first breath
and so, you don't get to
demand atonement in your second.
If I could,
I would lend you my eyes
for you to grasp why I am compelled

to tear up the ground you stand on.
Perhaps then our footsteps would align.
The way they did when I had to take extra steps to match your pace,
when you were the sun and I revolved around you and you and you.
I know it hurts you that I picked up my roots and reassembled them
into a language you don't understand.
I know you think me self-sabotaging,
but to me it is too offensive
to be a minnow in a net cast solely by men.
Subjugation grows so systematically in the branches
of your father's family tree,
you place such pride on the rebellion living in your blood,
until your blood picks up and rebels against you.
But maybe I was born to push your membranes further.
And since I was shaped to be outrageous in my defiance,
your outrage cannot bother me.
If I could,
I would be your little girl forever.
But you equipped me for battle,
the moment you taught me to cast my opinions in iron.
And since you made me so unbending,
I am no one's except my own.

IF MY BODY SPEAKS

I love the way you hold me when you hold me like we have no bones like each rib can come and crush together and melt into the sinews of the heart. I love the way you look when you're just looking introspective and unfocused eyes blend into unfocused thoughts – until you get caught and quickly rearrange a face you have grown to adore. I love the way you flatten our chest into the grass when we lie in lazy summer sunshine, and our skin fuses together into slow stickiness but we don't mind, we don't mind. I love the way you laugh when you laugh unguarded and unexpected, the way other laughs must rise to join us like some alarming bird-song in the otherwise quiet. I love the way you sleep when you sleep with our mouth open and the next morning wonder if a spider may have vacationed on our tongue, the way you peer at us in the mirror to examine each of our eyelashes, and split open a smile. I love the way you saw us at eleven years old, when you could have taken over every moment with how relentlessly you loved us, and you would have, you would have, I know you would have. I love the way you look at me when you look at me softly, when you gather me up and thank me for rebuilding us after times of momentary failure, when I fall apart somehow and keep us indoors, buried under a pillow.

Most of all, I love the way you slowly grow when you slowly grow unashamed of me. I know it is a stubborn mountain to unclimb, after years of understanding your body as a shortcoming, but I've loved you from the moment you had eyes with which to see us.

And I will love you without question, right up until the moment that they close forever.

ACKNOWLEDGEMENTS

This book would not exist without so many incredible people, and I only know a fraction of their names. To all those who have been working beyond my reach and behind the scenes to make my poetry a reality, thank you, thank you, thank you.

To my family, who hold me together at the seams. You have watched over me and loved me even at my most ridiculous! Thank you to my brother, who humbles me with his generosity. Thank you to my beautiful mother, who has taught me devotion, and to my father who has taught me resilience. And thank you, always, to my sister, who forgives me for my many mistakes. You are brilliant.

To Jamie, who has been patient and loving at every step of the way. Thank you for always saying 'of course' when I ask if I can read you my latest poem, and for stopping me from being too harsh on myself.

To my friends who have been so supportive and so excited throughout the process – thank you always, for your love. I have barely seen you all because of the pandemic we are still living through, but I can't wait to hug you all again! Thank you to Bea, to Simi, to Laura, to Nessi, to Becca, to Mhairi for reading my writing at some point or another and constantly quelling my fears. I love you.

To Calum, who told me to enter the competition which led me here. You keep saying you didn't do anything but it's not true – thank you for knowing my capabilities before I did.

To Tom who understood my writing from the beginning. I consider myself incredibly lucky to have worked with you. Thank you for teaching me how to write a collection, thank you for being my editor. (And please be my next one!)

To Abi who has championed me every step of the way, thank you for your reassurance and your guidance. And thank you to The Good Literary Agency for championing unheard voices.

To the #Merky team for all the incredible work you do. It has been such an honour to work with you – thank you for doing all the heavy lifting and making it seem so effortless. Thank you to the copy-editors, proofreaders, social media team, publicists, designers, illustrators, assistants, editors, event managers and many more who I am sure I have left out in my ignorance.

To my loved ones stretched across oceans, thank you for your memories, which have been keeping me warm. I'll see you soon!

To all the women who came before me, whether they were my own blood or other generations of artists, poets, writers, fighters, advocates, educators, survivors. My success was paved by your bravery and your wisdom. To the English teachers who nurtured me and to Derek Lennon, who predicted this.

Finally, thank you to Stormzy, who set out to create a publication that holds space for stories like mine. I am forever grateful to #Merky.